You
Take to the Sky

By Lisa Trumbauer

CELEBRATION PRESS
Pearson Learning Group

Contents

The Young Eagles Program Is Born

Imagine soaring high above the ground. Below, you can see forests and lakes, houses and shopping malls. From the sky the highway looks like a ribbon as it winds through the hills. You may even see your school or athletic field.

Airplanes give pilots and passengers a bird's-eye view.

Young Eagles receive certificates and badges to remind them of their flights. The pilots get special caps.

If you are a Young Eagle, you don't have to imagine all this. You will see these things for yourself.

An eagle is a bird that soars high in the sky. Young Eagles soar, too. Instead of using wings, Young Eagles use airplanes.

Young Eagles is a special program started by the Experimental Aircraft Association, or EAA. The EAA began in 1953 in Milwaukee, Wisconsin, as a group of pilots who built their own airplanes. Today anyone who is interested in flying, or aviation, can join the EAA. Its members include pilots, airplane owners, and people who build their own airplanes. There are about 170,000 members in chapters in all 50 states and around the world.

In 1991 the EAA was thinking about its goals for the future. It asked its members to offer ideas.

One goal came up more than others. That was to get children interested in flying. The next question was how to do that. Many members said that they first became interested in flying when a friend or family member took them for an airplane ride.

Young Eagles introduces young people to flying.

These ideas became a reality on May 13, 1992. That was when EAA announced that it would hold special Young Eagle Days. On those days pilots would offer free plane rides to anyone between the ages of 8 and 17. Today the Young Eagles Program introduces many young people to flying.

The EAA's aim was to give flights to 1 million children by 2003. That year marked the fiftieth anniversary of the EAA. It was also the hundredth anniversary of the Wright brothers' first flight.

One million flights in only a little over ten years is about 100,000 flights a year. That's a lot of flight time.

On December 17, 1903, the Wright brothers flew the first airplane near Kitty Hawk, North Carolina.

Most Young Eagles get their first flights in a small plane such as this.

The first Young Eagles Day took place in 1992 in Oshkosh, Wisconsin. Steve Buss is the director of the Young Eagles Program. "Since the program was launched," Steve says, "over 800,000 young people worldwide have experienced a Young Eagles flight."

The program is usually offered throughout the year. Programs at different airports may vary. Pilots from around the world volunteer their time and their airplanes taking kids for free plane rides. Today more than 31,000 pilots have given their time and airplanes to the Young Eagles Program.

Meet the
Young Eagles

Steve Buss explained several benefits of the Young Eagles Program. An airplane flight can help young people see their community in a new way. The program can also help get kids interested in flying. Children can also learn about some of the many possible careers in aviation.

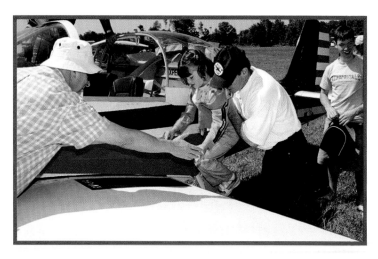

The pilot shows a Young Eagle where to step to board the plane.

Jamail Larkins decided to become a pilot after a Young Eagles Day.

Jamail Larkins is a Young Eagle who became a pilot. Jamail was 12 years old in 1996 when he had his first flight through the Young Eagles program. Taking off from an airport near Augusta, Georgia, Jamail remembers seeing his house from far above. He believes his Young Eagles flight gave him his interest in aviation.

Jamail explained that a few months after his first Young Eagles flight, he started taking flying lessons. He would not be able to solo, or fly by himself, until he was 16. Still he was able to fly with a pilot. He learned how to take off and land, how to turn and climb, and how to read the instruments on the control panel.

Drew Baird of North Carolina had a similar experience. "I took my first flight with my uncle, but never became truly hooked on flying until my first Young Eagles ride, nearly seven years later," Drew said. Like Jamail, Drew also began flight training and earned his pilot's license. Now 18, Drew even volunteers during Young Eagles Day, flying other kids for free. He began as a Young Eagle, and now he is teaching new groups of Young Eagles about something he loves—flying.

Young Eagles get to soar high above their neighborhoods.

Karrie Shanks took her first Young Eagles flight when she was 16. "It was a huge thrill," she said. "Everybody said I didn't 'land' for a week. I was so excited."

Today, at age 18, Karrie has her pilot's license. She also helps on Young Eagles Day. "The gift of flight is very special. I would love to share it with more people."

Young Eagles Day

A typical Young Eagles Day begins with registration. Would-be Young Eagles must come with a parent or guardian, who gives permission for them to fly.

You can feel the excitement as kids wait for the day to start. They can see the small planes waiting to take them up, and they wonder which one they'll be flying in.

The Young Eagles registration desk

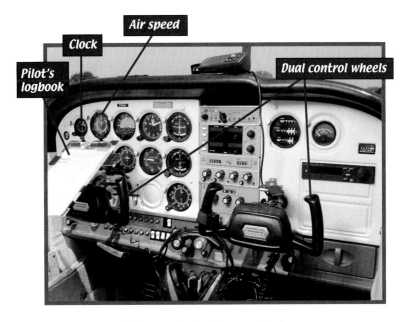

Air speed

Clock

Pilot's logbook

Dual control wheels

The cockpit of a small plane

Before the flight the kids attend a short class. They are introduced to the parts of an airplane, including its controls and instruments. The instructor goes over safety rules. Older children may be given a booklet with more information, such as radio communications, weather briefings, and a map of the airport.

Next the Young Eagles gather around the pilots and pair off. Each pilot walks a child to an airplane for the **preflight check**. Together they look at the engine to make sure they have enough oil. The pilot opens a cap on the wing, where the gas tank is located, to make sure they have enough gas.

The preflight check is important.

Checking the wings

The pilot invites the Young Eagle to feel the wings and the rudder. Together they make sure that the airplane doesn't have any cracks or dents, especially on the propeller. They also check the tires to make sure they have plenty of air. The airplane must be in good shape before it can fly.

Now it's time to get onboard. The pilot and the Young Eagle put on their seat belts and headphones. The headphones will help them hear each other and also talk with other pilots when they are flying. The pilot checks the instrument readings, which tell how high or how fast they are flying.

Finally the plane moves onto the runway. It waits for its turn to take off, then zooms down the runway. The pilot pulls on the control wheel. The control wheel is similar to a steering wheel that moves the plane up and down as well as from side to side. Now the airplane is in the sky!

During the flight the pilot points out things below. Like Jamail, the Young Eagle may see his or her home or school. Everything looks so different from way up in the air! From up above, lakes look like small puddles, and cars look like ants.

It's almost time for take-off.

A Young Eagle may even hold the wheel. There are two control wheels, one in front of the pilot and one in front of the passenger. All the time the pilot is in full control of the plane. The Young Eagle acts as a sort of co-pilot, getting the feel of the plane's movement.

The planes flown by pilots for the Young Eagles Program are small. Most small planes, such as the Cessna 172 or the Piper Warrior, seat only two or four passengers.

The Young Eagle may be the only passenger in a two-seater airplane. In larger planes, the Young Eagles can fly with their brothers, sisters, or friends. The small size of the plane gives Young Eagles a personal and up-close chance at flying.

After about 15 minutes or so, it is time to land. The new Young Eagles receive certificates and badges to remind them of their flights. Their names are entered into a special logbook that lists the names of all the kids across the country and around the world who have become Young Eagles. The EAA is very proud of the fact that the Young Eagles logbook is the largest logbook of its kind in the world.

Getting Involved

There are many ways for children and adults to get involved in the Young Eagles Program. One way is to go to a Young Eagles Day in their area. To find out when that is, children can call a local airport and ask. There are thousands of small, local airports all over the United States. Most participate in the Young Eagles Program.

This boy just earned his Young Eagle certificate.

Many small airports participate in Young Eagles Day.

Another way to find out about Young Eagles Day is to look through newspapers for Young Eagles announcements or check out the Young Eagles Web site. The Web site has lots of information about the program and you can find it at www.youngeagles.org.

EAA also offers a summer camp called the Air Academy, in Oshkosh, Wisconsin. It offers all sorts of aviation activities. At camp, Young Eagles may build a real airplane or learn about hot-air balloons.

Jamail Larkins attended the camp while he lived in Georgia. Georgia is very far from Wisconsin. No problem! The EAA Air Academy helps with some of the costs of attending camp.

At the camp Jamail met hundreds of kids his age who were interested in flying and aviation. He had many great experiences that he'll never forget. Jamail got to fly with Chuck Yeager, the Honorary Chairman of the Young Eagles Program. In 1947 Chuck Yeager was the first person to fly faster than the speed of sound. Perhaps someday another historic flight will be made by a Young Eagle!

Glossary

aviation	the work of flying airplanes
benefit	something that is good or helpful
controls	parts that control a plane's speed, height, and direction
instrument	a tool for doing very precise work
logbook	the full record of an aircraft's flight
preflight check	a check done by a pilot or mechanic before each flight to make sure a plane is in good working order
propeller	blades that rotate to make a plane fly
radio communications	communications between the pilot and an air-traffic controller on the ground or another pilot
registration	the act of recording information
rudder	a part that steers an airplane
solo	to fly an airplane alone
weather briefing	information about the weather that may affect a flight